KILL THEM BEFORE THEY GROW
THE MISDIAGNOSIS OF
AFRICAN AMERICAN BOYS
IN AMERICA'S CLASSROOMS

by Michael Porter

Chicago, Illinois

TABLE OF CONTENTS

> The Afrocentric strategy seems to be paying off
> academically. A recent study of 82 black private
> schools nation-wide found that over 60% of the
> schools' students were scoring above national
> averages in reading and math. At Ivy Leaf, a
> majority of students go on to top parochial high
> schools or public magnet schools.[1]

Lasting awareness---that in-depth understanding, which penetrates the superficial differences or similarities between theories and practice, that level of consciousness, which allows you to see the truth no matter how bitter, horrible, or controversial---often comes about gradually.

As I look back on elementary school, middle school, high school and university classes that were designed to help me become a knowledgeable student, teacher, and counselor, I see now that America's educational system promotes a system-maintaining curriculum, which virtually guarantees the oppressed remain oppressed and the oppressors remain oppressors. Some will say that school is what you make of it. I say that the American system of education is charged to make something of us.

During a conversation with a White male teacher from Students Exploring And Reasoning For Creative Horizons (SEARCH), there arose in my mind a lasting awareness about the nature of public and private schools (K-12). I have always known that most private schools are majority Caucasian and that the majority of African

American children are in public schools and that notable differences in opportunities are presented to each group. After our conversation, however, I realized that the problems are deeper than mere differences in opportunities. Let me explain.

The SEARCH teacher and I are literally on opposite ends of the educational spectrum in two significant ways. He's a middle-class, middle-aged, college educated White man. I'm a younger, oppressed-class, college miseducated African man. He teaches an "elite" group of Caucasian children who score highly on tests and are thus labeled "intelligent." All of my students are African and are considered rejects, trash-can material. Our differences laid the foundation for our discussion. I mentioned that the majority of African American public schools are negatively stereotyped and that, unfortunately, the stereotypes too often become reality. The SEARCH teacher believed the problems stem from classism as well as racism. He said that predominantly White private schools supply America's middle-class, while the public school system produces menial laborers and the hopeless. He stated this as fact.

The SEARCH teacher's belief can be debated from several perspectives, but I wish to view it in light of master-slave relations. Regardless of how much "progress" African Americans make, there is a basic superior-inferior, master-slave relationship that exists between Africans and European Americans. Based on the fallacy that Whites are normal and intelligent and Africans are abnormal and dumb, this relationship is built into the policies and culture of all Caucasian-controlled institutions. This is why Behavior Disorder classes and mentally retarded classes are usually filled with African Americans---males in particular.

America's educational system reveals so many truths about this society, especially in its treatment of African American boys. Whether our boys become productive, prosperous, noncriminalized men is a litmus test for public education. My experience as a teacher of children labeled Behavior Disordered proves to me that public education in America has failed the test. Measured against the condition of African American boys, public schools should be viewed as toxic. I am not saying that White private schools are better for African American boys; I don't have any experience teaching in White private schools.

This writing tries to explain how bright African American boys become casualties in public schools. African American boys are hosts upon which system-maintaining parasites feed. These boys are used as a source of income for a vampire colony of educated Whites and mis-educated African American professionals who worship the very theories that damage African American boys. These theories are effectively utilized by social service agencies, mental health agencies, and penal institutions. It is my hope that once this horror is comprehended, we, African American men and women, will take an action-oriented approach to CONTROLLING predominantly African American public school systems. I will offer recommendations at the end.

KILL THEM BEFORE THEY GROW is a wake-up call for those who don't know. This is a summation of my more than seven years of working with children labeled Behavior Disordered.

Throughout this book I use the proper nouns "African" and "African American" interchangeably. I believe it is crucial that we go back to calling ourselves "African" if we are to obtain the collective consciousness which is necessary for group survival. Since nobody was really concerned with what I taught to African boys during my first three years as a Behavior Disorders teacher, I used Jawanza Kunjufu's *Lessons From History: A Celebration In Blackness* (both *elementary and advanced editions*) as both a reading and social studies textbook. The young Brothers loved it (as did several teachers). Dr. Kunjufu's work convinced me that "African" and "African American" were the proper names for us. Many of us have forgotten that before we were negro, colored, and Black we were African. As you will read in the Recommendations section, identifying ourselves as "African" is crucial to our fighting and winning the war against White supremacy.

My heart has already gone out to my young African Brothers in those hell-hole "BD" classes. With this writing, I give more than my heart.

Michael Porter
Savannah, Georgia
February 8, 1997

Sheriff John Brown always hated me. For what I do not know. Every time that I plant a seed, he said kill it before it grow. He said kill them before they grow.

The Honorable Bob Marley in the song, "I Shot The Sheriff"

PUBLIC LAW 94~142 AND THE CREATION OF BLACK MONSTERS

Mentally retarded children were excluded from this nation's public school system for a long, long time. It took major lawsuits to force this nation's governing bodies to make educating retarded children mandatory for public schools. In 1975, Congress passed Public Law 94-142 which guaranteed that any United States citizen 20 years old and under has a right to receive a free public education based on his or her needs. This law mandates special education for all disabled children. Public Law 94-142, within itself, is excellent and just. However, as with many just things in a selfish, nonspiritual, racist society, they are often used for unjust purposes.

Public Law 94-142 created special education. Upon the creation of special education classes, there also arose the need, for funding and profit-making purposes, to increase the "market." As with anything else in American society, public school systems are big business. The best way to maintain or increase market share for any product is to create needs.

It is important that people view artificial needs as real needs; this way, people will feel that there is progress being made in society. The naive, unsuspecting public will come to believe that the problem "solved" by the product always existed but they, the public, were unaware of the problem's existence. This type of ignorance allows evil to flourish for centuries. Understand that new products, services or institutions are not necessarily signs of progress---especially in a capitalistic society.

Special education programs and classes became abundant under Public Law 94-142. The public became aware of, and accustomed to, terms such as "mild, moderate, and "severe retardation," "autism," and "dyslexia." The people whose jobs demanded knowledge of the meanings of these words became another group of education professionals, or special educators. Special teachers, psychologists, and psychiatrists became salespersons for special education. Shoe salespersons must sell shoes to remain in business; many special educators believe they must sell dysfunctionality to keep their jobs.

European and European American theorists found new life in special education. "Behavior modification," "token economies," "positive and negative reinforcers," "extinction," and many, many other terms which come from Caucasian men who sought to define reality or aspects of reality were up and running. Children now had to be found to fit some category of illness and abnormality. Almost every idiosyncrasy found in children became a potential "problem area" which could be improved or fixed with special education services. Create a disease and find someone to give it to. Textbooks had to be printed, college classes, seminars, and workshops had to be developed; new theories had to be created. In short, a special education industry was created.

In American society tests are law and gospel. If a test says a student is in the low range of intelligence, then he's declared stupid. If a test says a student is emotionally disturbed, then he or she is indeed emotionally disturbed. *Period.* After spending several years as an educational therapist, a child and family therapist, and now as a teacher in the Behavior Disorders program, I am personally and professionally convinced that all tests in America, especially standardized tests, are used for the following two reasons only: 1) To maintain the race and class status quo and 2) To enable agencies, schools, colleges, textbook publishers, and test making companies to make a profit.

Tests in Western society historically have been based on human deficiencies. The French Ministry of Education asked Alfred Binet, a psychologist, to develop a way to identify children who would not benefit (i.e., learn) from public education. The officials' purpose was to reduce or eliminate overcrowded conditions in the schools, not build upon the innate strengths of children.[1]

The year 1904 was just 39 years after slavery legally ended, and 28 years after Reconstruction. What was the reality of Africans in America in 1904? Jim Crow, lynchings, castrations, separate and unequal, old text-books, the Ku Klux Klan, the rape of African females by White men, the great African migration northward so we thought, to escape racism and find jobs. This was our reality during the time intelligence tests were created. Was African reality taken into consideration in Europe or America when intelligence tests were being devised? No. African people were seen by Caucasians as little more than monkeys, and Africa was a land of savages.

More than 90 years have passed since the French Ministry of Education asked Alfred Binet to devise his test. Not only have many changes been made to the tests, new ones have been created. There are now tests for almost everything. With so many tests in America, it seems strange that this nation would rank 30 out of 41 among industrialized nations in education.[2] Where do African Americans stand today in regard to standardized tests? We score lower than European Americans---regardless of which data you examine. Since Alfred Binet, there has been much debate about whether intelligence and other tests are culturally sensitive and fair to "minorities." While some culturally unbiased tests have been developed the reality of a society based in White supremacy is clear---NO TESTS WILL BE DEVELOPED WITH THE INTENT TO BENEFIT AFRICAN AMERICANS.[3]

Whites have never wanted Africans in classes with them or their children. White Americans never intended

4

for Africans to be in any kind of class except the slave class, despite our victories in court. Six years after the Supreme Court ordered immediate school desegregation (1969) Public Law 94-142 was passed to allow Caucasians a way to become desegregated and segregated at the same time. Their number one concern was the African male in America's educational system. Each African male in America was, and still is, perceived in the European historic mindset as a potential Marcus Garvey, Nat Turner, Elijah Muhammad, Malcolm X, Louis Farrakhan, W.E.B. Dubois, Henry Delany, and the like. Why is this so? Because Caucasians know that it's in the nature of men to be in charge of their destiny and the destiny of their people. White America cannot afford to have educated African men in their midst.

Thus, the American public education system made "Black male" synonymous with "disabled." This was done through the creation of the labels "Behavior Disorders" and "Emotional Disorders." These labels say that African boys can't behave without special treatment, juvenile probation, and, in many cases, drugs. This label condemns African boys to the very bottom of the educational ladder---few architects, teachers, business owners, doctors, or others will come out of BD classes. African boys have become public education's monster---feared, mistrusted, and hated, mere animals to be confined to cages (special education classes). In some school systems, every school has a BD class.

This is sophisticated segregation. Any group that attempts to desegregate a public school should learn from the mistake that the NAACP in Savannah, Georgia made. Our local NAACP simply focused on segregation and desegregation as it existed about 32 years ago and did not take into serious consideration the various programs' Whites had developed in schools which segregated children under such pretenses as SEARCH, Another Chance at Education, MAGNET, Severe Learning Disabilities, Other Health Impaired, Behavior Disorders, Mildly Mentally Impaired, and a host of other programs. Caucasians know that today African Americans are having serious problems understanding subtle, sophisticated racism. The 1970s have been called the decade through which African Americans slept. If this statement is true, then Caucasians were the first to catch us sleeping. While we were sleeping, our boys were being targeted for elimination. Now, Whites are creating schools for African boys called Alternative Schools. These schools are jokingly called BD schools by many educators. Why? Because these schools will primarily house African boys and girls. Who else is mostly labeled BD?

"For 12 years, civil rights enforcers said nothing about the way Georgia schools assigned students to classes. But in the past year, at least five Georgia districts, including Early and Evans counties, have faced the loss of federal funds for diverting students into advanced, average and slow classrooms in a way that federal investigators found had no legitimate educational purpose. In case

6

after case, Black children who outscored White classmates on standardized tests were steered into the low track anyway, investigators found. Meanwhile, Whites were elevated into the top classes regardless of low scores."[4]

Clearly, White supremacists in public education are determined to miseducate (destroy) the minds of African children, especially males. The above quotation also reveals one of the reasons I don't trust tests nor the test givers (examiners). I believe that we African Americans will never know the true genius of African children, because Caucasians are telling us which of our children are "normal" or "smart." Caucasians will never elevate African children to an academic level equal to or above Caucasian children REGARDLESS OF HOW HIGH THE AFRICAN CHILD SCORES ON TESTS.

"I think a lot of it is heredity, and these are the people who are here breeding," said Libby Swann, a special education teacher Turner County. "They stay here, they multiply here."[5]

Caucasians will stoop to the lowest level to place, and justify placing, African boys in special education classes. I believe African American adults would change for the better overnight if some Caucasian teachers and other Caucasian professionals were as openly honest as Libby Swann.

Probability of Special Education Placement

City/State	White	Black
Vidalia, Georgia	1:784	1:34
Magnolia, Arkansas	1:151	1:19
San Juan County, Utah	1:272	1:30
Geneva, New York	1:123	1:15[6]

The federal government cannot stop this madness. Every facet of American society works for the maintenance of the White supremacist system. African boys, especially, only mistakenly "succeed" in America's public school system. By the 12th grade, they are supposed to be ill-prepared and totally demoralized about staking their claim in this world.

The evil use of European and European American theories on African people is, and always will be, destructive for the Africans. Conquerors can't be trusted to truly educate the conquered. Caucasians will always push African boys and girls in a direction, which makes it easy to diagnose, label, and place them in BD Programs, youth detention centers, and mental health agencies--all of which function from the perspective that African boys are disabled and must be "helped." No help is forthcoming.

THE CONNING OF AFRICAN AMERICAN PARENTS

Before beginning, allow me to pose a question: How do you act in the presence of White people?

Since White people are THE standard of appropriateness, knowledge, wisdom, and beauty in this White supremacist society, is it any wonder that many Africans speak more British than the British when around Caucasian people? Is it any wonder that many Africans act mute in the presence of Caucasians for fear they won't "sound" right? Is it any wonder that many Africans agree with any and everything spoken by Caucasians when in their presence?

We have been reared to believe in and worship Caucasians, and this has had a detrimental effect on African people the world over, including Africans in North America. The belief that we are of little value while Caucasians are of maximum value prevents us from becoming self-actualized human beings. Self-actualized individuals have racial pride, confidence based in self-knowledge, and are productive. For too many of us, our self-esteem appears healthy when we're around one another but extremely lacking or non-existent when we're around Caucasians. Many of us become childlike when in the presence of Caucasians. We smile at damn near everything they say and are kind to excess. Whether acted on by medical doctors or unemployed dropouts, this pathological behavior has, to some degree, effected all of us. Having stated this, I will now discuss how too many African American parents are conned.

Con artists convince people to believe in them, and then to allow them access to something---usually money. Many Caucasian, and some African, teachers, counselors, principals, social workers, and psychologists con African American parents, especially mothers, on a daily basis. Money is not what the African mothers are conned out of. They are conned out of their children--especially their African sons and grandsons. The conning usually begins with one or more teachers, mostly Caucasian females, suggesting to the principal, counselor or special education teacher that a particular child be screened for a behavior disorder. The child is usually an African boy, and the school is usually an elementary school.

After the school staff has observed the child, the parent, usually a single African woman, is sent a letter to attend a meeting to discuss her child. The conning has begun. The school and special education staff have already decided that the African boy should be placed in the Behavior Disorders program. They are confident that they will convince the mother to sign the necessary forms giving them permission to test and place her son in the Behavior Disorders program.

The meeting. The African mother is lured unwittingly into the vampire's den where her son's life blood, spiritually and mentally speaking, will be sucked out of him. These teachers, counselors, and principals throw their titles out to the parent. Titles, I have found, intimidate many African American parents, especially if they are not college educated or do not hold a professional position that carries an impressive title. Like wolves sneaking up on their prey, these educational assassins use words the parent may not understand. To avoid appearing "dumb," the parent will usually agree to whatever is being recommended.

The assassins use phrases such as, "for the welfare of your child," The idea is to convince the already intimidated mother that they're on her side. They will ask the mother if she has any questions. If she asks any questions at all, they're usually insignificant.

The wolves close in. Pen and forms are passed around for all to sign, especially, permission forms for the mother. After the mother has unknowingly signed her child's soul away, the wolves become more aggressive. "You may want to consider having your child evaluated for medication" comes next. The grave is dug. The assassins will then introduce the "merits"of drugs, usually Ritalin or Mellaril, to the now overwhelmed African mother. They'll tell her that drugs will help her child focus more and make better grades. Such statements are hard for the parent to dispute because she usually knows nothing about Ritalin, Mellaril, or Attention Deficit Disorders with or without Hyperactivity.

By the time the parent leaves the meeting, she has signed her son's life away. She will take her son to see a medical doctor, usually one recommended by the assassins, to have medication prescribed. The grave is filled. This sad, life destroying scenario occurs over and over again. Although there are some African mothers who refuse special education classes for their sons, there are far too many who give in.

From here on out, the African boy exists within a maze of guinea-pigism and bureaucratic paperwork designed to keep him forever a BD student. The misguided, victimized African mother is simply mailed forms to sign which guarantees that her son remains an American educational casualty. He and thousands of his BD peers will be the source of income for mostly middle-class Caucasian women, the topic of many doctoral dissertations, and human guinea pigs for medication administered by state mental health clinics and private physicians. Today it's Ritalin and Mellaril. What's being planned for our children tomorrow?

PAYCHECK SLAVERY AND THE AFRICAN AMERICAN PROFESSIONAL

It is important that in this discussion of how and why African American children are placed in Behavior Disorder classes, we discuss the strange relationship many of our university educated administrators, teachers, social workers and psychologists have with their paychecks. This strange relationship is, in my belief, not only a problem affecting African American boys, but is one of the more serious problems impacting African communities in America.

We have believed that as more and more African Americans receive college degrees and obtain professional jobs with substantial salaries, they would elevate the race. We have believed that these high paid, well-educated Brothers and Sisters would become sources of inspiration for our youth and will open doors for the rest of us once they're "inside." But a strange thing happened on the way to the corporate suite.

The paycheck. Thirty years ago, a bullet to the head of an African American leader and his followers was enough to keep the rest of us in check. Today, however, assassination is too obvious. Enter the paycheck. The

high (sometimes not so high) digit paycheck has re-
placed the assassin's bullet that was meant to suppress
and eliminate African American leaders and potential
leaders. Too many Brothers and Sisters simply sell out.
The wholesale buying into of Caucasian and Western values has deadened the revolutionary perceptive ability of
too many African Americans. Instead of seeing White
supremacy, they see White dollars. This is really hurt-
ing us. Ironically, as perverted as it seems, it costs White
folk more to kill us than to buy us. We sell our dignity,
our integrity, and, God help us, even our souls.

After becoming accustomed to or enslaved by the
paycheck, the Brother or Sister becomes fearful of los-
ing it. The Mercedes Benz, two hundred thousand dollar
mortgage, charge cards, and all the trappings of The
American Dream becomes their very reason for living.
Because they become owned by what they own, they end
up with two masters: the Caucasian master with his or
her paycheck and their material "possessions." These
African Americans' greatest fear is the White man or
woman saying to them, "Nigger, give me my damn job."
Next, the African employee will hear, "Boy (girl), if you
want to keep your job, you'd better do what I tell you!"
In a total state of fear, professional African Americans
turn ruthless against any Brother or Sister who challenges
their White boss or the system the White boss represents.
Herein lies one of the greatest dangers to African American boys.

An institution's policies embody attitudes, philosophies, and other intangibles which, for African Americans, do a good job in camouflaging White supremacy. When conscious, caring African Americans rise up and question the policies and politics (usually racist) of the system, the Caucasians put the paycheck slaves out front to lead the assault. Many of these paycheck slaves will make brothers like Supreme Court Justice Clarence Thomas look like Nat Turner. They fight for the White supremacists' tooth and claw. They don't care that African boys and girls are suffering because of their owner's policies. They care only about their salaries and their image. Their reasoning reminds me of the confused mental processes of schizophrenics---it makes no damn sense. The African paycheck slave, however, could not care less if he or she seems schizophrenic as long as the master is satisfied. The hidden message behind most, if not all, American institutions is this: Keep the niggers down and out---if you can't keep them out, keep them down.

So, what can we realistically expect these institutions to do for our African babies? The very policies that should benefit them diagnose them, label them, and destroy them under the pretense of "helping" them. The same policies make it easy to place and keep African children in special education, BD classes while White children are placed in Learning Disability classes which carry no stigma. The African paycheck slave supports this genocidal practice.

When Caucasians see their African paycheck slaves being held up as "leaders" and "pillars" of the African American community, they lose what little respect they may have for us. Imagine just having been told that a conscious, African-centered Brother or Sister you know was marrying a Caucasian. Regardless of how objective you may try to be, you'll lose much respect for that Brother or Sister. As Whites observe our worship of African Americans who help to destroy our children, they become emboldened in their destructive activities.

African paycheck slaves usually have such titles as Director of Special Services, Minority Participation Director, Assistant Superintendent, Behavior Specialist, Counselor or Principal. They earn salaries ranging from sixty thousand to one hundred thousand for their role in destroying African boys.

It is necessary that all of us hold discussions about paycheck slavery---open, self-critical discussions. These discussions can give us a deeper sense of commitment and moral strength, which strengthens us in the presence of money and material temptations. Let's lose no more soldiers to the Caucasian's paycheck.

THE MYTH OF EQUALITY

Oppressed people become equal with their oppressors when they are no longer oppressed. To be oppressed is to be unequal---economically, educationally, in the job market, and otherwise. Many African Americans have confused image with substance. We believe we live in a free society, but the reality is, our rights could be taken away with the signing of a document---it's literally that simple. How does our believing in the myth of equality make us participants in the destruction of African American children in general and African American boys in particular?

Too many of us assume that most Whites view our children as equal with their own; therefore, we believe White teachers and other professionals will treat our children equally. Our ignorance blinds us to the destructive, racist, lopsided scheme that places African American boys into special education classes---Behavior Disorder specifically.

Believing the myth means that we believe our boys are inherently emotionally and behaviorally disordered. You can't believe one without believing the other. Whites take our self-destructive ignorance and hold it up to

17

show the world that we have agreed to being miseducated, labeled, and mistreated. When Whites see that we allow and condone the mental destruction of our future husbands, fathers, and leaders through Behavior Disorder classes, they feel justified in their mistreatment of us. Many Caucasians don't even view their acts as mistreatment. They see it as the natural order of things. Some may even think they're helping us.

One of the most pathetic individuals is the "educated" African American who argues his or her approval of having African American boys incarcerated, drugged, placed in special education classes, and, believe it or not, beaten by policemen. White society gives these individuals much positive exposure and placements on many committees whose agenda is often anti-African. Besides being miseducated, these misguided Brothers and Sisters (many of whom are paycheck slaves) have internalized self-hate to a frightening degree. For some of them, there is no turning back.

We must not let the desire for equality blind us to the horrors of inequality. Saving our boys from Behavior Disorders classes require a realistic perspective and a realistic approach. Special education classes often prepare our boys for youth detention centers and jails. This is reality. I have seen well-meaning Brothers and Sisters advocate for BD placement and medication for African American boys and girls. They thought they were doing the right thing. Today, however, many of them are beginning to see the truth and all the White supremacist horrors that come with it. Like myself, these Brothers and Sisters have become advocates not only for African American boys, but for African people everywhere. When you begin to see the truth you must preach it, practice it, and stand for it.

Some African Americans say that the majority of African American boys are alright--it's only a minority that's having difficulties. Let's not let naivete' blind us to the truth. There are obvious casualties and not-so-obvious casualties. We must cease basing our progress as a people on those of us who have "made it" despite racism. Our overall well being must be evaluated on how well our whole group is doing. Jews and other powerful groups do not determine their status as a people on the minority Jewish element, but on the majority Jewish element. Too many African American men are in prison; too many African American children are in special education classes; too many African Americans are unemployed; too many African women are raising children alone---these are the criteria we must use to determine how well-off we are.

An African American boy who has completed high school without ever having been placed in a Behavior Disorder program has not necessarily "escaped" the effects of racism. The answers to the following questions will determine how well-off these Brothers are: 1) Are they academically prepared for post-high school success (college, technical school)? 2) What track were they on in high school---general or college prep? 3) How many times were they retained during K-12? 4) Are they prepared to get jobs in highly technical environments?

School systems sell myths to parents just as Burger King sells burgers to the public. For example, some school systems try to sell the myth of racial equality through pictures of Caucasian and African children sitting side by side in a classroom. Many African Americans are fooled into thinking that they can trust that school system. As of this writing, the school system I work in has only 13,000 Caucasian students out of a total system population of 36,000 students (more than 22,000 are African American); however, advertising leads us to believe the system is 50-50. Many African American parents, believing the illusion and think their children are receiving a good ol' integrated education; that their children are being taught to compete with Caucasian children confront reality.

WHITE FEMALE TEACHER +
AFRICAN MALE CHILD =
CHALLENGE AND PROMISE

CHALLENGE AND HOPE

There are sensitive, caring White female teachers and there are insensitive, apathetic White female teachers. The same goes for African American teachers---some treat African kids right, some mistreat them. Before examining the challenging yet promising relationship possible between White female teachers and African male students, allow me to briefly comment on African teachers who mistreat African children.

Some African American teachers and administrators are very negative in their interactions with and in their views of African American male students. Although destructive, there is a different sort of madness with these Caucasianized Brothers and Sisters who dog out African American boys. Let me explain this before getting to White female teachers.

The African American teachers and administrators who help destroy African American boys are, literally,

21

possessed by the life threatening values of Caucasian society. Like Caucasians, they view African American boys as a worthless, criminal element that should be cut out of American society once and for all so that decent, God fearing people can live out their lives in peace. These possessed Brothers and Sisters usually live in predominantly White suburbs and have their children in White private schools. Their children tend to act like buffoons when around their White middle class peers. Worst than being a fool is not knowing you're being a fool when everyone around you know you are indeed a fool.

One of the philosophical foundations of American society is based on the belief that the African male MUST be perceived as criminal, sex maniac, mindless brute, ignorant consumer, and entertainer. It matters not that we have famous and wealthy African American men-- the collective White belief is that we are basically and eternally dysfunctional.

Since the successful oppression of a people is determined by the absolute subjugation of the men, African American men must be checkmated in boyhood to prevent them from growing up to challenge White supremacy in America (indeed, the world). To assure effective subjugation of African American men, Caucasian females must be programmed to view African males as dangerous savages. Collectively speaking, White men teach their women and girls to fear, hate, and distrust African males so that he, the White male, can justify his oppressive activities. Don't bother wondering if Caucasians feel guilty. They feel no collective guilt about the so-called Indians nor us. Some White folk evade and/or rationalize guilt.

The diabolical, anti-African social conditioning scheme created by a Caucasian male dominated system has failed in its attempt to condition all Caucasian female teachers to mistreat African American boys. Most Behavior Disorder teachers are White females; this will not change anytime soon because White females outnumber all other groups as education majors in college. We would prefer that African men and women made our boys into men; however, given the numbers, we must understand that White women are often placed in this role. And there are Caucasian females who do care and work very hard to help African boys.

Not all White women see African American boys as peculiar objects that need fixing, i.e., test them, label them, place them, drug them, theorize them, set up gimmicks to help them learn, and have them earn M&Ms. There are White female teachers who desire to help our boys become business owners, teachers, computer programmers, and engineers. There are White female teachers who do not perceive our boys as "Black dummies" destined for menial labor.

We must inform them of our expectations as they work with our boys. There's nothing like a room full of confused, innocent, needy young Brothers sitting under the tutelage of a person who does not know how to help them. The movie Dangerous Minds, starring Michelle Pfeiffer, presented a highly romanticized view of the Caucasian female savior of inner city youths. Such Jane of the inner city films contribute to negative stereotypes of Hispanic and African males. We must help these teachers help our boys. Most will be grateful for our assistance. In these rooms, one will often find an African American paraprofessional or teacher's aide. This Brother or Sister is often large in stature and is used to create an atmosphere of discipline. The African American paraprofessional usually communicates better and achieves greater academic success with the boys than the master degreed teacher, but due to lack of formal education, has no decision making power.

Some White female teachers join with White social workers, psychologists, and physicians to hold conferences and seminars on how to work with special students. We must demand and advocate for the inclusion of African-centered professionals, ideology, and methods in these conferences and seminars. Although there are White female teachers who are willing to advocate for African children, we African adults must be in the forefront. Help is so much sweeter when you're helping yourself.

Since there are more Caucasian female special education teachers than any other group, it is important that we examine their communication styles as they relate to African American boys. The relationship between White female teachers and African American boys is one of challenge and hope. The relationship spans centuries of trials and tribulations, misperceptions and fears, stereotypes and reality. I will describe several interactional styles of White female teachers. The first is the *People Person White female teacher.* People Persons truly believe that all children---African, European, Asian, and others---can learn, and she tries hard to help them learn. She does not disrespect African mothers and grandparents who have children in special education. This White woman is open-minded and, therefore, open to African-centered ideas and/or methods designed to help African children. She goes to bat for what is right and refuses to allow stereotypes to determine her beliefs or treatment of the children. People Persons can reeducate their peers to perceive African boys in a positive light. She can help erase stereotypes and the problems they bring to the classroom.

People Persons who teach children labeled BD have many success stories to share. Their compassion pushes them to motivate and encourage African children to seek higher ground. Their hearts go into their work. People Persons can help other White female teachers overcome mostly unconscious behavior patterns and beliefs that hinder their success in working with African male children. I believe such White female teachers can change; however, they must be educated about their fears, stereotypical thinking, and misconceptions concerning African people. Let me, in the spirit of helping, explain some of the habits of a minority of White female BD teachers who fall into four other categories: *Touchy-Feely, Plantation Mistress, Theoretician, and Missionary.*

Touchy-Feely White females constantly perform subtle anatomical examination on the African boy. This female, because of societal stereotypes of African men, explores fantasies---even if on a mental plane. She may consciously rationalize her actions as therapeutic but, the reality is, she is fascinated with Black skin. This female teacher will often pamper the young Brothers with constant hugging and caressing which undermines much of the good she tries to accomplish. Whether conscious or unconscious, her interest in African boys is sexual.

The Plantation Mistress has a hands-off policy. She really can't stand even being near her students, so she instructs her African paraprofessional to handle various tasks or situations. She is often conceited. Economic necessity pushed her into this intolerable, deplorable employment situation. She can't wait to change careers or simply find a better job. If this teacher will attend some serious workshops on African children and their learning styles, she may change her outlook. She must be taught to see the challenge and the hope.

The Theoretician is well versed in every eurocentric theory in existence. She religiously believes each theory, and she puts them into practice each and every moment of her interaction with African boys. Until she has a command of African-centered theories and philosophies, she will unknowingly treat the young African boys like guinea pigs. They will be bombarded with tests and tricks - formal and informal, token economies, rat-maze type games, and M&Ms. The boys develop good memory skills with this teacher but absolutely no critical thinking skills. This White female teacher may be the one most likely to adopt African-centered theories and recommendations to help her students.

The Missionary is usually the teacher who persuades African American parents to sign their children's lives away. Unintentionally, this White female can do much harm to African children. She is often a eurocentric extremist who believes her way is the right way! She may be hard to reach. The Missionary tends to believe in the system religiously. She believes that the system can do no wrong. However, when her eyes are opened, she may become a devout People Person.

After doing this, we must let school boards know that we want to help teachers work successfully with African children---those in special education and regular education classes. Every school should have access to conscious, serious Brothers and Sisters who are willing to run the school if necessary!!

White female teachers need to know that we expect our children to be exposed to learning materials and individuals which will promote mental and spiritual growth. I know for a fact that any teacher will treat a child much better than usual when adults are actively involved in that child's learning experience.

A CURRICULUM OF GENOCIDE

Genocide is the systematic elimination of a people, the killing of the life germ or seed. Even though physical death is the primary goal, the very essence of the person may be destroyed long before the body.

A mentality of death originates from feelings of nothingness and hopelessness. Only self-awareness can prevent the nothingness and give rise to hope. Self-awareness must be taught. A mentality of death must also be taught. The power to miseducate and kill or educate and let live comes with whomever does the teaching. Everyday in America, one group of children is being taught a death mentality while another group is being taught a productive life mentality. Allow me to relate to you an experience that I believe will help you understand.

For several months, I sat in two history classes, one taught by an African American male, the other taught by a Caucasian male. Both classes were located in a public school that was more than 90% African American. In the White teacher's class, I sat and listened as he taught the history of Europe, including the "discovery" of America by Christopher Columbus. He spoke of all the European "explorers" who "found" this and that element of the "new world." He spoke of "God, gold, and glory" reasons for exploring the new world. As I observed the class and listened to the lesson, I thought about how often I heard the African American students call one another "nigger," "whore," and "bitch." I thought about how these same Brothers and Sisters check each other about skin color and hair texture on an hourly basis. Then I asked myself, Why in hell are they learning European history when they still see themselves as "niggers?" This lesson was not helping to improve their self-image nor their self-awareness.

The self-image and self-awareness of the Caucasian children in this class, however, were being elevated, polished, and shined. These European American children were receiving a eurocentric education that was designed to maintain and advance European/Caucasian/Western values.

The African American teacher, on the other hand, taught world history. The textbook he had to use was an exercise in historic-schizophrenia to the point of being sickeningly humorous at times. In one chapter, the children were taught that the world's oldest civilization began in Asia. The illustrations were of Caucasians with tans. The next chapter described Egypt in a very mystical manner detached from Africa. African empires were barely discussed. This tricky, deceitful presentation of world history confuses African American boys and girls.

They never see the relationship between the ancient Egyptians and themselves and often perceive Africa in a less than positive light. The only time they are certain they're being discussed is when the book discusses the Western slave trade. What is significant here is that African American children are often taught that African people in general, and African Americans in particular, had no existence before the Western slave trade.

Such vague, distorted teachings about African people is deliberately planned, made mandatory for teaching, and implemented by the European Americans who control this nation's educational policies. From kindergarten to twelfth grade, most African American children are taught a curriculum that negates the achievements of African people. Are African American children who master this curriculum without knowing anything true and worthwhile about Africa and her people really "smart?" If so, one must ask, "Who benefits from these youths smartness? The mastery of such a eurocentric curriculum by African children who have no knowledge of self is merely an advanced form of programmed destruction. Sadly, some of these children will grow up to be used by Caucasians to work against the liberation of their African Brothers and Sisters; this is the true danger of the eurocentric curriculum. Like a bug spray, the eurocentric curriculum affects enough of us to have us go into our communities to spread the programmed destruction to our Brothers and Sisters.

After "successfully" going through this eurocentric curriculum, we all become somewhat behavior disordered. The curriculum teaches peoples of color to admire and respect White people while simultaneously holding themselves in contempt. After years of witnessing African American boys and girls walking through school halls and sitting in classrooms calling each other "nigger," "too Black," and "bitch," I have concluded that there are no merits whatsoever to a eurocentric curriculum unless you're Caucasian. Even though there are other reasons why we and our children call one another degrading names, schools can be used to help prevent and eliminate much of this insanity. After all, schools have a captive audience by law and instill perceptions in children from four to eighteen years of age. A lot of good or bad can be done to a child in such a large time frame. We'll deal with this in the section on recommendations.

MEDICATED TO LEARN MEDICATED TO ACT RIGHT: THE SLAUGHTER OF AFRICAN AMERICAN BOYS

African American boys are targeted for medication, incarceration, experimentation, and eventual extermination. It's amazing how Caucasians make money off African Americans while simultaneously destroying African Americans. It's as if America's economic structure is giving monetary incentives to those who are actively destroying Africans in America. If you're destroying African American males, you get extra bucks. It's amazing.

When I was a child and family therapist at a state mental health agency, I had a very interesting experience. One day while sitting and talking to one of the White male psychiatrists, the secretary buzzed his office and stated that someone had come to see him. I was about to leave but the psychiatrist said I could remain. I sat down. A well dressed, tanned, mousse-haired White man walked into the office carrying a rather large briefcase. After polite greetings the well-dressed White man placed the large briefcase on the psychiatrist's desk and opened it. The briefcase was a portable drug display case. This White man was a salesman for a pharmaceutical company. He explained two of the latest drugs to the very attentive psychiatrist. I was stunned.

My school has 830 children, 90 percent of which are African. When I go by the nurse's office everyday and observe the "medicine line," it seems as if 25 percent of the school's population is on medication---Ritalin, Tofranil and Mellaril primarily. When I watch the children tossing those pills down their throats, I think back to an experience I had at the mental health agency. One day I was looking through the *Diagnostic and Statistical Manual of Mental Disorders,* trying to find an appropriate diagnosis for a client, and the one that truly fit was under the category not related to mental disorders. I explained to one of the psychiatrists the diagnosis I wanted to use for this particular client and explained my reasons. The psychiatrist told me that he agreed, but that I couldn't use the diagnosis because the state would not pay for diagnoses under that category. Therefore, I had to make the person "sick" so that the agency could get paid. I wondered how many middle school children were on medication because of an ill-deserved "diagnosis" because some agency had to get paid?

The message children are receiving from being medicated is if there is a problem with their attitude or behavior there's a drug out there somewhere that can make things better. Children are given the message that it's unnecessary to experience stress, anger, or depression

because there are drugs to help one cope with these feelings. As these children progress into adulthood, they may
tend to view alcoholic beverages, cigarettes, and cocaine
as a kind of "medication" to be used for the alleviation
of social pain.

White people, as a whole, have a fondness for drugs.
Now White people are not drug addicts by nature; however, I believe that their fondness for drugs exists. because they have trouble feeling on a spiritual level.
Whether they believe it or not, many White people
use drugs to help them "feel" something of a spiritual
nature. They use drugs to escape this crazy, self-destructive materialistic monster they created---the same
monster that damages the lives of so many African
people.

Needless to say, my personal experiences with
seeing young Brothers consistently misdiagnosed and
overmedicated made me suspicious of agencies and
schools. I am, at this present time, somewhat paranoid
of Caucasian psychiatrists, psychiatric social workers
and nurses, counselors, psychologists, and certain teachers. I harbor a mixture of disdain and pity for their African counterparts. My paranoia is not without substan-
tive grounds.

> We have enclosed the violence initiative package
> you requested, concerning the federal government's
> racist project to identify young inner city children on
> the basis of biological or genetic markers.[1]

The above quote is the entire opening statement from a cover letter written by Peter R. Breggin, M.D., director of the Center for the Study of Psychiatry, and Ginger Ross-Breggin, director of Public Education and is part of the package which explains, in frighteningly graphic detail, the Federal Violence Initiative. The Caucasian politicians, doctors, and other experts who created the initiative could very easily be Adolph Hitler's first cousins. I find it interesting that African Americans are seeking equality in this nation while the White supremacist power structure simultaneously seeks a way to do away with us. The racist planners of our destruction have developed a deadly plan, which they feed, through propaganda, to the American public. The public is nudged into agreeing with the deadly plan.

There is a tendency to think superficially about theories and programs that are spawned from diabolical White supremacist think tanks. For example, everyone agrees that crime, especially violent crimes, is a serious problem in America and something must be done about it. In reality, our agreeing about crime stops at the mutual acknowledgement that it's a problem. The White supremacist power structure is attempting to resolve the problem by planning to kill African males. Obviously, African Americans cannot agree to this solution to crime because these African men and boys are our brothers, husbands, sons, fathers, lovers, and leaders. So the White supremacist power structure has to trick African people into approving our own death sentence.

According to the Breggins: "Currently, more than 4,000 children and youth in the United States are involved in funded studies examining biological markers and variables, cognitive deficits, and other supposed predictors of violent behavior."[2] This means that the White supremacist power structure will study the genetic make-up, intelligence test results, and damn near anything else that will help to prove that African males are genetically coded for violence, rape, drug addiction, school failure, gang membership, armed robbery, and drive-by shootings. These demonic Caucasian policymakers will create measurement devices designed to yield the results they want. We are killed under the guise of being "helped."

Breggin and Breggin became aware of the Violence Initiative when the press reported the remarks of a prominent and powerful White male psychiatrist named Frederick Goodwin. During his address to the National Mental Health Advisory Council on February 11, 1992, Dr. Goodwin compared young inner-city (code word for Black) males to violent, highly sexed Rhesus monkeys. Dr. Goodwin represents the views of many European Americans. Whites, such as the Breggins, who reveal the true nature of programs such as the Violence Initiative are viewed as extremists. During slavery, these Whites would have been called "nigger lovers." In Nazi Germany they would have been called Jewish sympathizers. It's not about liberal or conservative, upper class or lower class, it's about race. Collectively, the mental reasoning and basic views of Caucasians as it relates to African people have not changed. The consumer response to *The Bell Curve* is illustrative.

The Breggins do an excellent job of explaining the social-psychological dynamics which, when they exist in Europe or America, give rise to racist, destructive movements such as the Violence Initiative. Dr. Breggin explains that when social ills increase, the ills are "rationalized" in "biomedical terms that blame the victim..."[3] So, African male children and adults are declared genetically abnormal and useless and a burden to society. This destructive characterizing of African males, children in particular, carries with it the message that the American economy, educational system, standard of living, and criminal justice system will greatly improve if African males are disposed.

The Breggins explain that for programs such as the Violence Initiative to take effect, people must believe that it is politically and economically unfeasible to address the underlying economic, political, and social causes of suffering. The Breggins cite remarks made by Dr. Goodwin in which he explains his belief that a "large social engineering of society" is unnecessary and that the focus should be on "identifying individual vulnerability factors rather than large, rough cut, social demographic variance."[4] Frederick Goodwin fully understands that focusing on REAL CAUSES of crime and other social ills would indict America and its racist practices. This psychiatrist understood that the VICTIMS must be blamed, but for this blame to take place, the victims must be perceived as perpetrators. Racism is tricky. Focusing on improved housing conditions, economic development, educational change, and equity in the workplace would be too much like *rights*.

According to Dr. Goodwin, to engage in effective victimizing, "the targeted individuals must be seen as physically and mentally abnormal and experts must be able to identify the defective persons."[5] Since African American men and boys are the primary threats to Caucasian men, it is crucial to the well-being of American society that we are biologically identified as some type of freakish, dangerous, perverted, mentally deficient savages who will destroy this civilized White nation. Our genocidal oppressor "measures" the degree of intelligence in African American children, knowing quite well that most of them will score below Caucasians on culturally bias tests. They then use their European culture-oriented tests to say that something is wrong with our children. Next, they recommend a drug legal or illegal as a cure or remediation. It is only a matter of time before psychosurgery (physically altering parts of the brain) is openly offered as the best treatment for "correcting" the behavior of African boys in particular, and all Africans in general.

Now, one could say that if some of the loss of social structure in this society, and particularly within the high impact inner city areas, has removed some of the civilizing evolutionary things that we have built up and that maybe it isn't just the careless use of the word when people call certain cities jungles, that we may have gone back to what might be more natural, without all of the social controls that we have imposed upon ourselves as a civilization over thousands of years in our own evolution.[6]

What Dr. Goodwin is saying in the above quote is that certain groups (Africans specifically) are uncivilized and that the areas we live in (inner cities), are "jungles." This racist psychiatrist is implying, in not so subtle terms, that African Americans are causing societal regression in the United States. In other words, European Americans are in danger as long as there are uncivilized, savage African Americans running around in this country's "jungles." This belief causes extreme Caucasian paranoia which leads to profound mistrust of African American males. The welfare of their little White children is in jeopardy. Tax dollars are being wasted. The savages must be eliminated!

Our children don't stand a chance against this governmental-medical-pharmaceutical beast. As we give our precious African children over to Caucasians to be taken care of, they truly will be taken care of! We must see *some* non-Afrocentric mental health agencies, non-Afrocentric psychiatrists, non-Afrocentric psychologists, non-Afrocentric social workers, non-Afrocentric counselors and non-Afrocentric teachers as premeditated MURDERERS of the African community. Africans also must view *some* of our own people in the so-called social service and help professions as White supremacist assassins. If this view seems too extreme for you, it is because you truly don't understand what is taking place. Today it's Attention Deficit Disorder With or Without Hyperactivity and Conduct Disorder and Socially Maladjusted and Emotional-Behavior Disordered and Mildly Mentally Handicapped. Today it's Ritalin, Tofranil, Prozac, and Mellaril. Tomorrow it's psychosurgery, zombie pills, guineapigology and psycho-laser castration.

I don't believe the conditions of suffering people "naturally" get better. Things often get worse. Take a look at the turn of events for Africans in America: slavery, Reconstruction, Jim Crow, civil rights, and today's civil rights backlash---things don't "naturally" improve. The White supremacist power structure knows things don't naturally improve, and this is the reason they are moving against Africans so systematically. They thoroughly understand what Dr. John Henrik Clarke repeatedly calls the "essential selfishness of survival."

African American boys are targeted for medication, incarceration, experimentation, and eventual extermination. What else do you expect America to do for them? Educate them to run this country? Teach them to become Xerox and IBM executives? Help them become President of The United States? Help them become business

41

owners or bank presidents? Educate them to run hospitals? Help them become surgeons and architects? What do we expect White America to do for African children, especially boys, when we send them to school?

Hitler, regardless of what you may think, was not an anomaly. His cold-hearted, ruthless, murderous philosophy is inherent within a larger Caucasian mindset. Hitler could not have killed six million Jews without the support of the German population. Slave owners could not have killed upwards to 100 million Africans without the support of Europeans.

A COMMENT ON MULTICULTURALISM

Because so many people of color are demanding the inclusion of their contributions in this nation's educational system, we now have what is being called multiculturalism. This is a joke. When Europeans conducted a takeover of indigenous nations, they didn't plan on one day having to "include" the conquered in anything except that aspect of life which was designated to the oppressed, conquered people. Inclusion leads to power. Power leads to self-determination. Self-determination means you are no longer oppressed. The White power structure will have none of this. Multiculturalism is the White power structure's attempt to pacify those who wish to be "included."

I have run into many African American and Caucasian teachers who believe that a multicultural curriculum will help build the self-esteem of African students and, thereby, lead to improved academic performance. The assumption is that fairness exists in the minds of the Caucasian writers and historians. However, when it comes down to rewriting the curriculum, many African American teachers find that Whites, generally, agree to change very little. Few Caucasians are open to having facts about African and African American people made known to an entire city's school system. The Caucasian children and parents may become upset; the African children may become angry after learning all the White lies-- this is Caucasian rationalization. Some Caucasians have an inherent fear of Africans knowing the truth about what they did to us. They fear repercussions even though they know we don't control the military or have a militia. It's hard for most Whites to admit that Egyptian civilization which included science, mathematics, and literature preceded Greece.[1] It's hard for most Whites to admit that the founding fathers of America where racist slave owners.

Throughout history, Caucasians have exploited many cultures. Sure, they may patronize Mexican restaurants, eat Chinese food, enjoy watching ten Black basketball players, and name athletic teams and auto-mobiles after so-called Indians, but they view this as entertainment and symbols of Caucasian conquests. African people often mistake the liberal gestures of some White people as a sign that they are sincere about helping others.

A good friend, Omar Imhotep, has stated that the purpose of multiculturalism was to benefit and empower White women. He believes that multiculturalism will ultimately lead to a unisexualization of the school environment and, consequently, the effeminization of African boys. Some Whites think multiculturalism is honoring certain groups in a particular month. We now have Black, Hispanic, Native American, Asian, and women's month. The remainder of the year and throughout the above months, schools continue to teach White male supremacy.

44

WHY DEBATE AFRICENTRICITY?

There should be no debate.

A sure sign of pathology in some African Americans is their disagreement with African-centered anything. Our blind, wholesale acceptance of any and everything European is sick. Many Brothers and Sisters who disagree with Afrocentricity have absolutely no problem acknowledging and believing in White Santa Claus, a Caucasian Christ, White fairies, and, in general, White people. They view their pathology as OK.

Caucasians debate and disagree with Afrocentricity because they are either ignorant of African history and African American accomplishments or they are aware of African history and African American accomplishments but are afraid to approve of African American children learning about African people. Collectively, Caucasian people are comfortable and secure with African people being ignorant about themselves. Whites know that self-awareness motivates people to become self-determining. Self-determination in a people erases self-destructiveness---Whites need us to be self-destructive. We are no threat to their power as long as we exhibit self-destructive beliefs and actions.

They do, however, play games with us. School systems and agencies often work collaboratively to obtain government grants to work with "at-risk" groups---i.e., African American men, women, and children. The grants address issues such as AIDS awareness and prevention, teen pregnancy, job skill development, and crime prevention. After obtaining the funding, these agencies and school systems do the same old eurocentric things they've been doing for decades in their work with "at-risk" African American boys and girls. The result of these eurocentric programs is very poor. Occasionally, a "success story" will be promoted to the public. If African-centered programs were funded to help African American children deal with AIDS, teen pregnancy, job skills, and crime, this would ensure much greater progress. In *The Isis Papers: The Keys To The Colors*, Dr. Francess Cress-Welsing mentions that under racism (White supremacy), grants will not empower African Americans because they go against the global domination interests of White supremacy.[1] For two years I worked with an agency that owed its existence to a multi-million dollar grant. What amazed me about this grant for "at-risk" youth and families (overwhelmingly African American) and the agency was the vast number of Caucasian consultants contracted to provide expertise. African-centered ideas and suggestions were considered too radical or unfeasible, and they were usually rejected. This multi-million dollar organization simply became a head-counting, number manipulation agency. I believe Dr. Welsing is correct.

Adopting a philosophy of Afrocentricity is a crucial step in reclaiming our rightful place on this planet. I know from experience that the African centered approach works best with African children. I have seen the eyes of African boys and girls light up as they were taught about their ancestors dating back to 4100 B.C. Our children love learning about themselves. They love learning that there is no difference between them and the Brothers and Sisters of their glorious past. They love seeing the pictures of the statues of our people's accomplishments. Their attitudes and behavior begin to change for the better. African American adults who frown at Afrocentricity do not understand this. Many of these professional African American men and women do not understand the miseducational reality of little African girls and boys learning everything about England, Spain, Germany, Italy and France but nothing about Kemet, Cush, Ta-Merry, Ghana, Mali, or Songhay. What they do learn about Africa is a bunch of lies and half-truths. When Whites see African Americans fight to have African American children learn about Europe and European Americans and simultaneously fight against anything Afrocentric, the Whites know we are successfully held in check, and soon to be checkmated.

Just think about it! Our children can learn about Dr. Martin Luther King, Jr. but not Akhenaten, George Washington Carver but not Imhotep, Harriet Tubman but not Hatshepsut---it's ridiculous! The White supremacy controlled educational system does not want African American children to see a connection between themselves and ancient or modern Africa. They want us detached. This strategy on the part of Whites started during the European slave trade. Confuse, divide, and conquer has been the successful strategy.

"These Black kids must learn to live with other groups" is the statement most often made by professional African Americans as an argument against Afrocentricity. The idiotic belief behind this statement is that if you teach African American children "Black stuff" they won't be able to co-exist with Whites because the "Black stuff" will cripple them. However, learning "White stuff" will help them to understand and enable them to work with White people (increase acceptance by Caucasians). This is nonsensical. When are we going to learn something that will enable us to work with each other and not call each other nigger?

Molefi Kete Asante states, "Afrocentricity is the centerpiece of human generation. To the degree that it is incorporated into the lives of the millions..., it will become revolutionary. It is purposeful, giving a true sense of destiny based upon the facts of history and experience."[2] The Afrocentric approach is necessary for the true and proper education of African children. An educational diet of Caucasian people and accomplishments is deadly for the African mind. Our children need Afrocentricity to live.

48

PRE~INCARCERATION

Mrs. Georgetta Blair-Simmons, a very insightful, strong-willed African woman who works with me, once stated that Behavior Disorder and In- School Suspension classes were designed to prepare African American boys and girls for prison life. She believed that Behavior Disorder and In-School Suspension classes were basically holding cells designed to house African American children until they were either old enough to go to jail or they committed a serious enough felony to be incarcerated. Let's look deeper into Mrs. Blair-Simmons' theory.

In his four volume series *Countering The Conspiracy To Destroy Black Boys*, Jawanza Kunjufu explained the fourth grade failure syndrome and the disproportionate number of African American children in special education classes.[1] We must stop and think for a moment: Where are the Irish American boys? Where are the Italian American boys? Where are the German American boys? Where are the Jewish American boys? Where are the Korean boys? The Japanese boys? The Chinese boys? They are definitely not crowding Emotional Behavior Disorder classes, In-School Suspension classes, youth detention centers, jails, funeral parlors, and graveyards. They are being "educated" to seize power and run America and the world. Our little African boys will be the source of income for many members of the other groups mentioned. Our little African boys will go to their stores to buy the latest jewelry, designer clothes, and athletic shoes. Our little African boys will be their clients in American criminal courts. Our little African boys will be the patients who receive their "medications."

The American educational system has no intention of truly educating African American children. Power is the goal of American education---power to create enterprises and employ your own people, power to not have to beg philanthropists and governmental bodies for money, power to free your sons and daughters from the promise of a life of juvenile detention cells, jail cells, and premature deaths. Real power!

In a country where the public educational system is becoming more non-White in terms of student population, and more Caucasian in terms of teaching population, African Americans are in for a very rude awakening. We tell our African babies to get a good education in order to get a good job, but seldom, if ever, do we stop and ask, "Who will give them this good education?" Only a realistic, painful look at reality and then doing something about it can help us. The issue is not that there are some well-meaning White teachers. The issue is that African American children, as a whole, are literally catching hell in this nation's schools. We don't have enough success stories. We will never have enough success stories as long as we expect and wait on a people who, collectively, have a superiority complex.

Placing Mrs. Blair-Simmons' theory on a national or global scale begs the question, "Is it possible that the public school system by design, become fodder for the nation's jails, mental health centers, prisons, and detention centers?" Remember, a system is called a "system" because independent entities work interdependently with each other for common objectives. The "system" has never been kind to African people.

I believe that the criminal justice system (courts, jails, prisons, youth detention centers) and the mental health system (psychiatric hospitals, mental health agencies, pharmaceutical companies) will soon play a MAJOR role in America's public education system. I believe they will become so intermingled until it will become difficult to determine where one ends and the other begins. Entire schools will become psychiatric-pharmaceutical laboratories. The trend is toward "full service" schools. I am reminded of the number of children crowding the nurse's office every class period for their daily dosage of Ritalin, Mellaril, etc. African American children, especially boys, have become the target market for the powerful mental health establishment. They already were the target-market for the criminal justice system.

As you read this, there are Caucasian females and males being educated in colleges and universities to work with African American students, clients, and patients. They will have few if any African centered professors who will properly prepare them. These individuals who work with (really against) our African boys and girls, derive their income from our "sickness." They have a vested interest in keeping our babies "sick."

The effectiveness of this theory will be revealed by the degree to which African American adults buy into new psychiatric diagnoses and eurocentric theories on causes of crime, misbehavior, and any other social concern. Whites sell us theories and ideas in the same manner and with the same effectiveness with which they sell us designer bags, shirts, shoes, and jewelry. They are absolutely assured of us buying into their definitions when they get various African American "experts" to preach the life-saving merits of the Caucasian's recommendations. African Americans must question any and every theory, new medication, new law, or anything recommended for our children.

THE MISBEHAVIOR OF SOME AFRICAN AMERICAN BOYS

It is true that some African American boys manifest rebellious and aggressive behaviors in school. Sometimes they are only verbally abusive. The result, however, is usually the same: suspension, expulsion, special education placement, or referral to alternative school or juvenile detention. There are reasons some of our African boys act up at school. These reasons must be comprehended by all who either rear or work with African American male children. Comprehension will at least stimulate some thought on the behavior of some of our boys. Let me first mention, that I don't use the word "children" loosely. We are talking about children, not men. This racist, white supremacist European American society has deliberately planted the picture of any and all African boys (children) as MEN whether they are 10 years of age or 100 years of age for this reason: *THIS LABELING GIVES THE MESSAGE THAT THEY "KNOW" BETTER AND ARE ABSOLUTELY TO BLAME FOR CRIMES OR THEIR OVERALL AWFUL CONDITION.*

Adults have the ability to choose their actions. So, when an adult performs a criminal act, the assumption is that he or she made a conscious, deliberate decision. When a 12-year-old African American boy is flashed on the six o'clock evening news, he is presented as a 12-year-old "man" in essence. As a result, you want this 12-year-old to be severely punished, not rehabilitated, because "he knew better." White supremacists want us to see African American male children as men. Ironically, apart from this labeling the white supremacist society views all African males as BOYS. They label us according to their plans for us---which are always harmful.

The first age range is daycare through kindergarten. My experience as a counselor and an educational therapist has shown me that life goes relatively well at this stage for most African American boys. They are generally spunky and full of confidence. There seems to be somewhat less television viewing and more curiosity-oriented, make-believe type of play, which is healthy. Although their African self-image is being harmfully impacted upon by the white supremacist society, they still tend to keep a sense of competence. But, they can only withstand the impact of white supremacy for so long.

The second stage is age 6-12 where the greatest harm is done to African American children. White supremacy is in full-effect. Upon entering first grade, most African American children are introduced to a 12-year European journey that glorifies Europe and white America while literally ignoring or down playing Africa, Africans, and African Americans. Snow White, Cinderella, Beauty and the Beast, Goldielocks, George Washington, Thomas Jefferson, King George, France, Italy, England, Britain, Cortez, Plato, Edgar Allen Poe, Queen Victoria, Emerson, The Boston Tea Party, The Revolutionary War, and a slew of other Caucasian personalities and events. When Africans are mentioned, it is usually in reference to slavery---not before. What does this have to do with industry versus inferiority? Simple---African children are not given the type of knowledge necessary to make them industrious; the information African American children receive in school mostly gives rise to feelings of inferiority. How can you expect an African child who is only taught about the glory of European people to acquire the motivating passion of self-help (industry)? It will not happen.

What kind of personal goals will the totally miseducated African American child set? To be an NBA star, an NFL star, a rapper, or to acquire a "good job?" They don't see themselves being mathematicians, diplomats, producers, philosophers, writers, doctors, or entrepreneurs---they see Whites achieving those careers. So, what is the result? They eventually lose interest in school. School becomes alien to them. They see no connection between the classroom and their future. They begin to specialize in socializing, PE, and lunch.

Older Brothers and Sisters often compare the children of the '80s and '90s to themselves when they were children (in the 1940s, '50s, and even '60s). They mention that they would, upon doing wrong, be spanked by a neighbor and would receive another spanking when they arrived home. Many of these older Brothers and Sisters comment that they didn't have an African-centered curriculum and they came out fine. When the majority of these Brothers and Sisters were children (1940s, '50s, and some '60s), they had caring, loving African American teachers who believed in them and held high expectations for them. Some of the teachers lived in the students' neighborhood. Most, if not all, of these teachers were spiritually grounded. They talked to students about life issues that would help them survive in this racist America. Also, when these older Brothers and Sisters were children, our neighborhoods were more like family---we cared about each other instead of deeply fearing each other the way we fear teenage African American boys today. We don't spank them anymore, we dial 911 instead. Very little of the safety net that was in place during their time exists today. When we adopted the selfish, individualistic values of white people we became lost. I don't believe we really understood the value of what we had.

The ages of 12-18 are a time confusion, between childhood and adulthood. A time for testing limits, for breaking dependent ties, and for establishing new identity.

Major conflicts center on clarification of self-identity, life goals, and life meaning. Failure to achieve a sense of identity results in role confusion.[1] Since the African American child has been fed a mental diet of white skinned, blue eyed, blond haired heroes and heroines, what type of identity do you expect him or her to have? Jawanza Kunjufu has mentioned that we are a people who are and have been called by many names. We have confused identities. Some of them tell me they are not African (when they call one another nigger, I tell them we are Africans, not niggers). A confused, miseducated African child either does not set goals or sets very unrealistic goals. When an African American child can tell you more about European and European American explorers (invaders and killers), diplomats (liars and thieves), and presidents (white supremacy's gatekeepers) than they can about the great achievements of Africans and African Americans, that child will suffer an identity crisis.

Knowledge of self is important for our children more than ever before since we don't have the past support system. Our children must not grow to adulthood simply to become clients, inmates, patients, and consumers. From day one, the American educational system encourages Caucasian children to take charge and run the world, while simultaneously teaching the African child to sit back and allow the Caucasian child to run the world. An African child needs an African diet (curriculum).

A confused adolescent becomes, in too many instances, an even more confused adult. They then become parents, send their children to be miseducated, and the process of mental destruction through mental slavery repeats itself into the next generation. Although I'm discussing misbehavior in school, which is erroneously viewed and treated as criminal behavior by many principals and teachers.

The following quotation is very enlightning:

> The Black-on-Black criminal's imagination is heroic. His heroism is cut whole- cloth from the white heroes he imitated as a child and adolescent man: the ones he saw in the comics, cartoons, movies and read about in the newspapers....who were always White. He uses their lingo, their cars, exaggerates their dress, spends their kind of money, kills with their weapons and with their heartlessness. He is a cartoon playing itself out in real time---a man acting like "the man" (White man). When he acts, he acts with a White man's image in his head as a model: copying boyhood heroes and villains. Now, as then, he and the white hero he imagines himself to be are one.[2]

Literally, many of our children's minds are not their own. How can they know how to act in school when the school's curriculum is toxic to their very essence as an African child? The African American child is, through the school's curriculum, encouraged to be white. The message from the Caucasian and European-centered curriculum goes like this: "If you want to be somebody, you better be white."

58

BEHAVIOR MANAGEMENT THROUGH SELF ~ KNOWLEDGE

In January of 1995, I made a comment to the local print and television media that an African-centered curriculum is necessary to change the problematic behaviors of African American children in the public school system. In response, a Caucasian editor wrote an editorial that claimed curriculum has nothing to do with the inappropriate behavior of students. I found his comment typical of most Caucasians and, sadly, even some miseducated African Americans. When it comes to problems plaguing African American people, Caucasians seldom are prevention-oriented. They become extremely defensive when Africans recommend solutions independent of White approval. The message Whites are really sending when they exhibit such attitudes towards African people is this: "You niggers are not smart enough to know how to help yourselves." Moreover, they have absolutely no intention of helping us help ourselves.

It has been my experience that too many Caucasians have trouble dealing with the whole child (body, mind, and soul). One child will have to be tested by a psychologist, then a teacher, evaluated by a psychiatrist, examined by a nurse, and then assessed by a social worker. They tend to be medical and behavior oriented and believe that African children are the cause of their own problems. Each child is no more than a file in several people's offices, to be evaluated and "treated" at varying intervals until he or she gets "better." These children are really being conditioned to become lifetime clients, patients and inmates for the vampiristic social disservice system.

"Point system," "rewards and punishments," "earned privileges," "staying on-task" are approaches designed to help BD-labeled students. These approaches are enthusiastically discussed in meetings, mostly directed by White females, held to discuss how to help the students. What we have is a classic case of White women teaching other White women and a few Brothers and Sisters eurocentric madness on how to "manage" African boys. I always feel strange in these meetings. One of the many tragic consequences that come from these White female "experts" is that some of the African American male Behavior Disorder teachers DO ONLY and EXACTLY what these White women teach them. The lack of self-knowledge prevents many of our Brothers and Sisters from truly helping African boys and girls get out of Behavior Disorder classes.

How can self-knowledge bring about disciplined behavior? When greater than a million Black men came to Washington, D.C. October 16, 1995, and there were no incidents of crime. Suppose that European American children, from kindergarten to college graduate, were NEVER taught about King Ferdinand, Leonardo Da Vinci, Socrates, Plato, Aristotle, Alexander The Great, Winston Churchill, King George, the Wright brothers, Christopher Columbus, Magellan, Alexander Bell, George Washington, and all the heroes of European history? How would they act? Suppose there were no European or American fairy-tales, only African American fables. How would they act? Suppose these White children, from kindergarten to college, were only taught about Menes, King Zoser, Thutmosis III, Imhotep, Hatshepsut, Ramses, Akhenaten, Nefertiti, Sonni Ali Ber, Marcus Garvey, Elijah Muhammad, Martin Luther King, Winnie Mandela, Nelson Mandela, and other African heroes, past and present? How would these White children act?

They would become detached and turned off from the information. They would become alienated because the curriculum itself alienated them. Many of them would become disruptive as a natural response to having something forced upon them---even if they believed in its "truth." Not only would the White children act up, they will begin to despise their people. Most Caucasian children would not do well in school because alienation prevents academic success.

Humans respond favorably to the truth about their individual group or race. In other words, all people do well and feel well when they have knowledge of self. I once heard Dr. John Henrik Clarke say that the Japanese were able to rise to prominence after being bombed in World War II because their self-confidence and concept of God were rooted in their own culture. If America's public education system wanted to help African American boys and girls behave and perform well at school, African and African American information would be infused into the curriculum, beginning in kindergarten. From a broader perspective, Africans and Europeans will NEVER be able to live together peacefully as long as Whites continue to prevent Africans from learning about themselves.

THE NEED FOR AN AFRICAN DEFINITION OF EDUCATION

Since the majority of African American boys and girls attend public schools, and since the public school system is controlled by the Caucasian power structure, and since the Caucasian power structure is, collectively, racist, African Americans must develop a collective definition of education that relates specifically to African Americans. This much needed collective definition of education for African Americans must be based on our reality and our real needs. This definition must not be apologetic.

Even though the outcome of education is supposed to be a good job, there is a critical difference between the validity of this goal for African and Caucasian students. The White child, consciously or subconsciously, inherently knows that "something good" is waiting for him or her. White children know that they are being looked out for. By the time a White child reaches fifth grade, he or she already believes the world belongs to White people. The seeds of arrogance are planted in Whites as children; the American educational system instills this master-of-the-world arrogance. It perpetuates the status-quo---which means it perpetuates the problems of African American children, women, and men.

Many people do not understand that when an African American child and a Caucasian child are sitting side by side in a classroom, two experiences are occurring. Whites are being educated to be rulers and Africans are being miseducated to be servants. The lack of a collective definition of education by African Americans makes this possible. African Americans make the serious mistake of believing that the eurocentric educational process can actually work for African children. So, we pass on the lie that our children should get that good education in as to obtain that "good job," but, our children know better. They may not know exactly what's wrong, but they know something is wrong. If we have a generation of lost African American children, it is because too many African American adults are floundering.

We must develop a collective definition of education. What is our reality? What do we African Americans need? We are an oppressed people mentally, economically, physically, and spiritually. We need African centered, African owned, and African operated schools, businesses, and security forces. To get these things, we must have a generally accepted African definition of education which we instill in African children pre-school through high-school.

Let me briefly explain my rationale for stating security forces as one of our needs. I know this scares many African Americans. It's sad that many African Americans believe that they can somehow "nice" their way into Caucasian acceptance; these Brothers and Sisters have surrendered their self-determination to Whites. Whether these African men and women realize it or not, they are telling Caucasians that they don't mind---and in fact they welcome---being impotent. They accept and offer themselves as NOTHING! ZERO! The mark of men is manifested by their willingness and ability to protect and defend their communities. I said community and not family because we must start viewing our community as our family. This view must force us into action. We need trained Brothers who keep our communities safe. Women and children will develop a profound respect for African American men. The symbolism of our action may be more powerful than the activities of the security forces. We must revive our ability to protect ourselves. I have always respected European Jews saying "never again" to the holocaust. Jews protect Jews, and likewise, Africans must protect Africans like never before.

Since education perpetuates culture, our definition of education must be just that---OUR definition of education. Every aspect of education and its vehicle for carrying it (i.e., the curriculum), must be culturally based.[1] African people must agree upon a definition of education that takes into consideration our ways of feeling, thinking and doing. And remember, our definition must not apologize for its Africanness.[2] There's a certain beauty and strength in not apologizing for being yourself--- especially a "self" that has been taught to hate itself.

Thus, I offer the following African definition of education: The lifelong process of using African-centered spirituality, critical thinking,and group protection to bring about self-determination for African people.

This definition can be embellished, but I believe it provides a good foundation. As you may notice, this definition mandates that we have self-awareness *before* entering school. This is significant because it places the responsibility of obtaining self-knowledge and self-awareness on our African shoulders. This early African education will, when it catches on, negate the oppressor's attempts to miseducate our children. I know this will not be easy, but it is absolutely necessary.

We need African and African American churches, fraternities, sororities and grassroots organizations to ALL agree on the definition and then plant it in all the African lives they touch, all the African ears they speak into, all the African minds they influence. This is the essence of our life and death struggle under White supremacy.

We cannot believe that other people's definitions of education apply to our African reality simply because they read and sound good. Their definitions are rooted in their culture, and they negate the significance of African and African American culture.[3]

Simply put, the European-based educational system, especially in America, sees you and me as abnormal and, therefore, unworthy of being culturally acknowledged. We must, with God's Help, take matters into our own hands.

RECOMMENDATIONS

African Americans must own, operate, and control our own schools, and we must have substantial control over public schools that have significant numbers of African American boys and girls. This control of public schools must focus on budget, policies, and staffing. Here's how it can be done.

Gaining Influence In Public Schools

After receiving several calls from distressed African American parents, teachers and principals, I organized a group of African American men to address these concerns. The only criterion for being a part of the group is that you're African and you care about African people. The group should openly discuss and identify problems that exist in the public schools which negatively effect African boys and girls. Don't become bogged down in a lot of philosophical debate; however, it is healthy and necessary for all issues to be debated before strategies are developed. Once the group has chosen its first two issues, members should set up a mandatory meeting with the superintendent and the president of the school board and present their concerns. Plan to schedule two meetings: in the first, your group will present its concerns, and the second will allow system officials an opportunity to explain what they plan to do about the problems. Beware: They will say things that sound good and show you things that look good. Get as many parents, grandparents, and foster parents involved as you can. These individuals are usually tax payers and registered voters; this can force local political officials to assist the group.

Organize a community-wide meeting. During the meeting, have the main speaker candidly state to the audience that an African American boycott of the school system may be necessary if the needed changes are not made. The collective African American community must be ready to deliver. One of the more progressive, aggressive ministers in my city, Reverend Bennie Mitchell, once stated to a radio listening audience that White folk only respect violence or a loss of money. I agree with him. Boycotting a school system causes a tremendous loss of money. Area churches and individuals can help with the placement of children during the boycott.

Budgetary and staffing demands should definitely be on the agenda. Research your system's budget and decide a percentage that must be spent with African Americans. African owned and operated businesses, including bookstores, dry cleaners, gas stations, consultants, construction companies, business or office supplies companies, band instruments, and computer stores should be given an opportunity to conduct business with the school system. Part of the budget should go to an African male teacher and principal training and recruitment program that is designed to work with young Brothers from first grade. Although teaching salaries aren't attractive to men in general, corporate downsizing (firing people), the international relocation of American companies, and America's struggle to compete with Europe, Japan and the Pacific basin countries, is providing a high quality pool of skilled, talented Brothers. Most African men enter the teaching profession because they need a job; however, given training and exposure to young people, they will soon learn to enjoy teaching. These Brothers should be aggressively recruited. Once your demands have been made, monitor the superintendent and school board closely. Don't be foolish and relax after giving them your list of demands.

You may have noticed that I didn't say much about African school board members. Let me explain. Some school systems have assertive Brothers and Sisters sitting on the school board. These African men and women fight for their constituents because they truly care about African children and parents. They don't cringe in fear of Caucasians. If your city has such a school board, then 50 percent of your work is still done because, joined with you, they become more powerful. However, if all or most of your African school board members are sellouts, your organization must view them as the oppressor, and proceed in an aggressive manner to get something done. The point is, you must do this with or without support from the school board.

Hold a press conference and a large community rally to generate support. At the press conference, the group should state its concerns, review the progress of meetings with the school board and superintendent, and present a list of recommendations. The rally, which should be planned at least two weeks in advance, must be fiery, well attended, open to the media, and held in an African church! There should be several very good speakers who charge and inform the audience about the issues being addressed by the group. The press conference and rally should put pressure on the school board and superintendent to address the concerns of your group.

Creating Our Own Schools

Our ultimate survival depends on our creation of businesses and schools and community security forces. The politics will follow. There is power in teaching your own. The issue is not money; the issue in starting our schools is willingness. We must be willing. How do we do this? Through the African church. If African American churches can raise millions of dollars to build bigger and better churches, then they can be called upon to build schools. New buildings can be built and old buildings can be renovated. Start small with 50 to a 100 students and build a good reputation. Create a board for the school and staff it with African entrepreneurs, as well as social workers and teachers. If nine people are on the board, five should be businesspersons and four should be Afrocentric, assertive professionals who know how to work with African children---this is a serious combination. The school must be marketed properly in newspapers, on radio, and throughout the local church network.

The curriculum must be African-centered. An African-centered curriculum builds self-awareness, self-esteem, a good self-image, and self-motivation. Fortunately, if your school needs a curriculum, there's African American Images in Chicago, Illinois which developed SETCLAE.

A Message To African American Parents

Do the following things:

1. Visit your child's school at the beginning of the school year and once a month thereafter. Meet with teachers and principals and have your child present. Keep high and realistic goals for your child and your child's teachers. Always let teachers know what you expect from your child and from them, and remember to have your child present when these discussions take place.

2. Make sure your child does homework everyday, even when he/she says the teacher didn't give any. Explain that gaining knowledge is crucial to becoming a self-sustaining adult and that you won't be around forever to take care of them.

3. Allow no more than two hours of television a week. Television, especially commercial television, does absolutely nothing to prepare African children to handle life; and since television is controlled by White supremacy, your African child will NEVER receive anything from it designed to help him or her her handle life effectively and productively. Television simply turns your child (and you) into a mindless consumer who benefits Caucasian merchants.

4. Talk with (not at) your child everyday. It doesn't matter if you have to wake them up an hour early--- MAKE TIME TO TALK WITH YOUR CHILD! No excuses accepted. "Tell me about your day," "what did you learn in school today?" "How are you and your friends getting along?" If you are not used to talking with your child, simply ask basic questions and LISTEN to what your child says. Never dismiss any statement your child makes as "stupid." Remember, if you don't talk to your child someone else will!

5. Remove all White Biblical images from your walls and Bible and explain to your child that it is important that we understand the truth about the people mentioned in the Bible because God is The Essence of Truth Justice, and Righteousness. Teach your child to pray after you have taught him or her that Jesus and the original Hebrews were African. We cannot afford to have generation after generation of African children growing up praying to a White savior.

6. Teach your child about money. Start with house hold expenses. Show and explain to him/her the gas bill, electric bill, water bill, mortgage or rent, and other expenses. Explain that money must be used on these things and that money must be saved. Explain that people "want" more things than they can afford and then explain the difference between "wants" and "needs." Also, explain the reasons you must save money and stress the importance of saving. Explain to your child we Africans make other people rich.

7. Talk to your children about male and female relationships. Tell them to respect themselves and not call each other "bitch," "Ho," "freak," "skeezer," and "nigger." Tell them that when we disrespect one African we disrespect all

Africans. Talk to them about AIDS, Herpes, and other Sexually Transmitted Diseases. Be straight up. Explain to them that sexual activity can have dire consequences. Rent videos on AIDS and watch them with your child. Tell your boys that they are not men simply because they can impregnate a female---tell them any fool can do that! Teach your daughter that becoming pregnant does not make a girl a woman. Explain to her that some males try to trick females. Don't sugarcoat anything because the consequences are too grave.

Start with these seven things. No matter how tired you are, do this. Don't make excuses; this is life or death. Make these seven practices part of your routine; make time everyday to do these regardless of holidays, events, TV programs, housekeeping, or visitors. Doing this requires NO MONEY, so make no excuses.

We've been celebrating Kwanzaa in Savannah, Georgia for the past five years. We do a full seven day celebration in an inner-city gym. I love Kwanzaa. Although Kwanzaa is not a religious holiday, there's something very spiritual about it. The seven principles of Kwanzaa (Nguzo Saba) are so very significant to helping African people help themselves that I must conclude this writing with a listing of the Nguzo Saba. I thank

Kwanzaa's founder, Dr. Maulana Karenga. Peace, Blessings, and Good Health to all of you.

NGUZO SABA
(The Seven Principles

1. Umoja (Unity) To strive for and maintain unity in the family, community, nation, and race.

2. Kujichagulia (Self-determination) To define ourselves, name ourselves, create for ourselves and speak for ourselves instead of being defined, named, created for, and spoken for by others.

3. Ujima (Collective Work and Responsibility) To build and maintain our community together and make our sister's and brother's problems our problems and solve them together.

4. Ujamma (Cooperative Economics) To build and maintain our own stores, shops and other businesses and profit from them together.

5. Nia (Purpose) To make our collective vocation the building and developing of our community in order to restore our people to their traditional greatness.

6. Kuumba (Creativity) To do always as much as we can, in the way we can, in order to leave our community more beautiful and beneficial than we inherited it.

7. Imani (Faith) To believe with all our heart in our people, our parents, our teachers, our leaders and the righteousness and victory of our struggle.

Dr. Maulana Karenga
7 September 1965

REFERENCES

Introduction

1. U.S. News and World Report. December 9, 1991. *"The Exodus"* pp. 66-77.

1 Public Law 94-142 and the Creation of Black Monsters

1. Allen, L. And Santrock, J.W. *Psychology: The Contexts of Behavior*. Brown & Benchmark Publishers. Dubuque, Iowa.1993.

2. USA Today. September 7, 1994. Page 1B *"U.S. Economy Reclaims Lead in World Arena."* By Bill Montague (USA Today).

3. Allen, L. And Santrock, J.W. *Psychology: The Contexts of Behavior*. Brown & Benchmark Publishers. Dubuque, Iowa. 1993.

4. The Atlanta Journal, The Atlanta Constitution. Sunday, Dec. 11, 1994. Pages G1, G4, G5. *"Who's Smart Who's Not" Sidetracked into Special Education*.

5. Ibid, pp. G1, G4, G5.

6. Ibid, pp. G1, G4, G5.

7 Medicated to Learn, Medicated to Act Right: The Slaughter of African Boys

1. Breggin, P.R. and Ross-Breggin, G. *The Federal Violence Initiative*. Center For The Study of Psychiatry, Inc. Bethesda, Maryland. 1992.

2. Ibid.

3. Ibid.

4. Ibid.

5. Ibid.

6. Ibid.

8 A Comment On Multiculturalism

1. Rawlinson, G. *The Egypt of Herodotus*. African Classical Studies Reprint Series Edition, 1990. ECA Associates. Chesapeake, Virginia. 1924.

9 Why Debate Afrocentricity?

1. Cress-Welsing. F. *The Isis Papers: The Keys To The Colors*. Third World Press. Chicago, Illinois. 1991.

2. Asante, M.K. *Afrocentricity*. Africa World Press, Inc. New Revised Edition. 1988. Trenton, New Jersey. 1988.

10 **Pre-Incarceration**

1. Kunjufu, J. *Countering the Conspiracy to Destroy Black Boys (Series)*. African American Images. Chicago, Illinois. 1994.

11 **The Misbehavior of Some African American Boys**

1. Corey, G. *Theory and Practice of Counseling and Psychotherapy, 3rd Edition*. Brooks/Cole Publishing Company. Monterey, California. 1986.

2. Wilson, A.N. *Black-on-Black Violence: The Psychodynamics of Black Self-Annihilation in Service of White Domination*. Afrikan World Infosystems. Brooklyn, New York. 1990.

13 **The Need For An African Definition of Education**

1. Nobles, W.W. *The Infusion of African and African American Content: A Question of Content and Intent*. Taken from, Infusion of African and African American Content in the School Curriculum: Proceedings of the First National Conference October 1989. Aaron Press. Morristown, New Jersey. 1990.

2. Ibid, pp. 5-24

3. Ibid, pp. 5-24

NOTES

NOTES

NOTES

NOTES

NOTES

NOTES

NOTES

_____

_____

_____

_____

_____

_____

_____

_____

_____

_____

_____

_____

_____

_____